Mother Teresa
Angel of God

Mother Teresa: Angel of God

Eugene Palumbo, S.D.B.

Resurrection Press
An Imprint of
CATHOLIC BOOK PUBLISHING CO.
Totowa • New Jersey

Dedication

To my mother who, in some small way, reflected the spirit of Mother Teresa in terms of concern for others and an abiding awareness of the presence and power of God in her life. The sickly and the suffering could always turn to Josephine Palumbo and know that she was there for them.

An indefatigable worker, she still managed to turn her thoughts to God, making prayer a part of her work. At home, whether preparing supper or cleaning house, she could, with disarming simplicity, offer short prayers to God.

Like Mother Teresa, she knew what it meant to suffer. And, like Mother Teresa, she knew how to make her sufferings a stepping stone to our heavenly Father.

First published in August, 2000 by Resurrection Press, Catholic Book Publishing Company.

Copyright © 2000 by Eugene Palumbo, S.D.B.

ISBN 1-878718-59-2

Library of Congress Catalog Number 132730

Inside photos: p. 27, Archdiocese of Newark; pp. 47, 57, 68 © Servizio Fotograpico de "L'O.R.," 00120 Citta del Vaticano

Cover design and photo by John Murello

Printed in Canada.

1 2 3 4 5 6 7 8 9

Contents

Foreword   7

Preface   10

The Young Agnes   12

An Interior Command   18

Houses for the Dying   28

Travels Abroad   36

Gifts from Many Sources   42

Leading Ministries   52

European Foundations   58

Champion for Life   64

Let's Do Something Beautiful for God   69

Death for God's Angel   73

Foreword

EVERYONE in the world, it seems, knows something about Mother Teresa of Calcutta. Everybody who has access to the media, certainly, as well as untold numbers who have been embraced by her, cared for by her Missionaries of Charity, or influenced by her words of wisdom.

Mention Mother Teresa's name and people listen. She has taught us by her life and so her inspiring words have a persuasive power beyond their simple beauty.

Mother Teresa was who she was and accomplished what she did because she believed God had a plan for her and a plan for everyone in the world. Everyone is good, everyone is important. Mother Teresa didn't believe in coincidence or chance. She manifested a faith that only a contemplative can embrace unconditionally.

A priest who gave retreat talks to Mother and her Sisters in Calcutta said that, at the conclusion, Mother said, "Father, pray for me." The priest reacted the way any of us would, and replied, "Mother, pray for you? I need you to pray for me!" And Mother Teresa said, "Well, let us pray for one another that we do not get in God's way."

God's way, God's will, God's plan, however we think of the eternal mind of our Creator, Redeemer and Sanctifier, after all is said and done, is the only thing that matters. "Thy will be done," Jesus taught us to pray. To know God's will, we must pray. To have the courage to respond to God's will, we must pray. To persevere in our response to God's will, we must pray.

Mother Teresa, known by so many as a woman of action was so much a woman of contemplative prayer that her works of mercy were prayers in themselves. She taught us that charitable works are not substitutes for prayer but the fruits of prayer. Without a loving union with God, our good works can only go so far. Just look at where Mother Teresa's love of God took her and how much she accomplished for multitudes of impoverished and afflicted people throughout the world.

Mother Teresa did just what Jesus did and taught us to do; she put the unconditional love of God and the unequivocal love of neighbor together. To live in the same age in which a fellow member of the human family, a Catholic religious woman, so closely imitated Jesus is an extraordinary privilege. You can't help but feel that she embraced with her whole heart and soul what many of us grasp only with our minds: that

Jesus though he was the eternal Son of God, became one of us so that we could fashion our lives after his. Jesus told us that the way to know him was to learn about His loving heart, meek and humble.

Mother Teresa talked about love as much as Saint John the Evangelist and she spoke about Mary as often as any of our Blessed Mother's most ardent children, few, if any of them more persuasively than she. If she seemed to have daily conversations with Our Lady, it is undoubtedly because she did.

We can be extremely grateful to Father Eugene Palumbo for giving us a beautiful portrait of Mother Teresa of Calcutta, a welcome biography, but much more, a fine insight into why she has become the best known and most influential woman of the twentieth century.

Most Rev. Frank J. Rodimer
Bishop of Paterson, NJ
June 2000

Preface

A TINY, frail nun stood before a distinguished gathering that included the King of Norway, high officials, and an enormous battery of photographers, TV crews, and journalists. It was December 10,1979, and the Aula Magna (Great Hall) of the University of Oslo hardly looked like a comfortable setting for the slightly-bent, sari-clad nun. Everyone waited for Professor John Sannes, chairperson of the Nobel Peace Prize Committee, to make his speech presenting the winner of that year's Peace Prize.

Citing many reasons for the committee's selection, Sannes said "respect for every individual's worth and dignity" was the hallmark of the honoree. "The loneliest, the most wretched, the dying destitute, the abandoned lepers were receiving from her warm compassion, devoid of condescension, based on reverence for Christ in man. Hers was a life of strict poverty, long days and nights of toil, a life that affords little room for joys other than the most precious."

When the prize recipient was invited to make her acceptance speech, she nervously clasped her award and the $192,000 prize, and stepped forward to the microphone to declare that she was accepting it "in the name of the hungry, of the naked, of the homeless, and of all who feel unwanted, unloved, uncared for throughout society."

Thunderous applause greeted the words of Mother Teresa of Calcutta, God's Angel.

Popular Winner

The selection of Mother Teresa as the recipient came as a welcome and refreshing change from the selections preceding her. It was felt that political considerations had influenced the choice of earlier winners. For example, in 1971, German Chancellor Willy Brandt was honored with this award. Critics found this selection terribly flawed and undeserving. In 1973, Henry Kissinger, United States Secretary of State, met with a similar disapproving response. The following year, Anwar al-Sadat and Menachem Begin fared no better.

A sumptuous dinner usually followed the award ceremony. But Mother Teresa convinced the committee to omit the dinner that year, and to use the money that would have been spent to provide an excellent dinner for 15,000 poor people in India. Mother Teresa frequently said that God works miracles for the poor every day. This was another occasion when her trust in the Lord was richly rewarded.

The Young Agnes

The world would be a much better place if everyone smiled more. So smile . . . be joyous that God loves you.
—Mother Teresa

Early Years

She had come a long way from the time and place of her birth: either August 26 or 27, 1910, in the small town of Skopje, the capital of what is now Macedonia. Of the town's population of 25,000, Catholics formed a very small minority. Her father, Nikolas Bojaxhiu, was a building contractor and served as a member of the Town Council. Her mother, Dranafile Bernai, hailed from Venice, Italy. Both parents treasured their three children and provided them with a happy, prayerful home. Named Maria Teresa at birth, Mother Teresa was given the name of Agnes at her baptism. Her sister, Age, was born in 1904, and her brother, Lazar, in 1907.

Many years later, Mother Teresa wrote: "I was always close to my mother. She was a holy and happy person who taught us to love God and our neighbor. We spent many hours in prayer in our parish church of the Sacred Heart, kneeling before the statue of Our Lady of Letnice, or late at night in our home."

Her mother and father loved the poor, and on several occasions provided a night's shelter and a warm meal for the homeless. Agnes was learning a lesson that would mark her later life in faraway Calcutta, India.

Active Parishioner

As a teenager, Agnes became very involved in parish activities. She joined the Sodality of Our Lady and the parish choir, often singing as soloist at Sunday services. During this time of her life, she showed great love for children of the parish and enjoyed giving them religious instruction. Through her pastor, Father Franjo Jambrenkovic, she learned about the Jesuit missionaries from Yugoslavia who had gone to India in 1924. The stories of their experiences filled her with a strong desire to chose India as her field of work as a nun. She eventually heard of the Sisters of Loreto who conducted schools in Bengal.

Call of the Convent

Years later, Mother Teresa wrote: "At eighteen years of age I decided to leave home and become a nun. From that moment on, I never had a doubt about my decision," she said. She pointed to heaven and exclaimed, "He made the choice!"

When she informed her mother of her decision, the saintly woman retreated to her room and remained there for twenty-four hours, deep in prayer. When she came out, she took her daughter by the hand and said: "Put your hand in His hand, and walk all the way with Him."

Her words did not fall on deaf ears.

Off to Ireland

Agnes wrote to the Sisters of Loreto in Bengal and was advised to apply to their regional office in Rathfarman, Ireland. There she would begin her study of English and her basic training for her work in Bengal.

Agnes, accompanied by her mother and sister, left Skopje for Zagreb by train on September 26, 1928. After a few days, Agnes said a final, tearful farewell to her mother. It was the last time that she would see her.

From Ireland to India

Settling down in Rathfarman, she made her first contact with the English language. It was a difficult course of studies, but she proved to be an apt and enthusiastic student, and in November 1928 she set sail for India, a journey of seven weeks. After spending a few days in Calcutta, she was directed on January 16 to the novitiate of the Sisters of Loreto in the mountain resort of Darjeeling, four hundred miles north of Calcutta.

There she began her life as a novice, attempting to familiarize herself with the spirit of the Sisters of Loreto, improve her knowledge of English, and receive some on-the-job training by teaching the poor children of the area. Her companions say that she fell in love with that sort of work immediately. She had worked with children in her home parish in Skopje; she had shared her mother's work with the poor of her home town, and this new setting for her work proved to be no problem whatever.

First Vows

Taking one's first vows in a religious society is always exciting and challenging. It opens up a new area in one's life, with brighter and wider horizons. A significant goal has been achieved, but much more lies ahead for the new Religious. On March 24, 1931, at the age of 21, Agnes pronounced her vows of poverty, chastity and obedience. A traditional practice in most   religious congregations recommends the changing of one's name. As the newly professed leaves behind many things of one's former life, the change of name symbolizes a fresh start in life with a new name, usually that of one's favorite saint.

Agnes chose the name of Thérèse in honor of Saint Thérèse of Lisieux. However, another nun had selected that name the year before, and there was some concern that confusion might result from the duplication. Agnes showed some creativity by deciding to use the Spanish spelling for her name—Teresa.

Early Assignments

Her first assignment was to St. Mary's School in Calcutta, where she remained for seventeen years, first as a teacher, and later (1937) as the principal. Her favorite subjects were catechism, geography and history.

Teresa took her final vows—a permanent commitment to religious life—on May 24, 1939, and was assigned to Saint Mary's as the religious superior. She now became known as Mother Teresa. Sisters under her direction described her as very selfless, one who radiated kindness and goodness in all that she did. Her role as superior did not create any illusions of greatness and power. For her, being in charge meant being at the service of others, as Christ Himself had taught His followers. In keeping with her deep respect for the poor and the downtrodden, she saw in each of her subjects the face of Christ, or as Professor Sannes would later express it, she saw the face "of Christ in man."

Those who worked with her recalled her ready sense of humor and her capacity to enjoy a hearty laugh with her Sisters. Said one nun, "She would hold her waist in both hands and thoroughly enjoy a contagious laugh when hearing a humorous incident or joke. She knew that a sad saint is a sorry saint."

Equally impressive was her life of prayer. The lessons she had learned from her saintly mother came into play throughout her life. At prayer she was a model of fervent concentration. Nothing could distract her from her awareness of the presence of God in her life. Her face, her eyes, her whole demeanor reflected her union with God.

— 2 —

An Interior Command

We must allow God to use us as He sees fit.

Lord, lend me Your heart so that I can love You as You love, and serve You as You served.   —Mother Teresa

The lives of the Sisters of Loreto became seriously affected by the events taking place in the world at this time. Powerful rulers in Europe and in Japan were reshaping the world's maps, and millions of people were killed or driven from their homes during the 30s and 40s. India, too, was caught up in this whirlwind of terror and destruction. Shortly after the outbreak of World War II came the Great Famine of 1942-43. All the river craft that could have served to transport rice from upcountry to Calcutta were requisitioned by the military.

The shipment of rice from Burma came to a complete halt as a result of the Japanese invasion. In the hinterlands of India peasants began to sell their land, and to flock to Calcutta to avoid starvation. The Bengal government was totally powerless in the face of these difficulties.

As hundreds of thousands of people invaded the city of Calcutta, they found no place to live.

Untold thousands died on the streets and in the alleys of the city. As the war progressed, matters worsened. The Indian National Congress focused its attention on the efforts to win freedom from Great Britain. As a result, bloody riots between Hindus and Muslims broke out, lasting for four days and nights.

A New Mission for Mother Teresa

For Mother Teresa and the Sisters of Loreto, as well as other religious societies working in Calcutta, this tragic state of affairs threatened them and their mission. The fate of hundreds of children in their care hung in the balance. Likewise, the area around Saint Mary's School degenerated into a frightening ghetto where the homeless and the hungry faced inevitable starvation and death. This critical situation posed a special challenge for Mother Teresa. Could she continue to work in a school where children of the wealthier classes were effectively shielded from the harsh realities of the life around them? Could she ignore the hundreds of thousands of people who roamed through the city seeking food and shelter, never finding anything to ease their plight?

In her heart Mother Teresa sensed a "second call" from the Lord. She had responded enthusiastically to the first call that directed her to share in the work of the Sisters of Loreto. Now that "call" was leading her in an entirely different direction. Like Saint John Bosco in the nineteenth century (1815-1888), who saw thousands of youngsters drifting through the streets of Turin, Italy, victims of the Industrial Revolution, Mother Teresa saw Calcutta's homeless, hungry, and neglected citizens in desperate need for someone to care for them. How could she rise to the occasion?

Answering the Second Call

In one of her many recollections about her life Mother Teresa once wrote: "The message to leave the Sisters of Loreto was quite clear to me. I felt God wanted something from me. He wanted me to be poor and to love Him in the distressing disguise of the poorest of the poor." Her spiritual adviser, Father Celeste van Exem, remarked: "For Mother Teresa it was not a vision. It was a communication that came as a form of inspiration. She felt distinctly that she had to leave the Sisters of Loreto and start her own work and gather around herself Sisters equally committed to the cause of the poor. Mother Teresa never doubted for a moment the reality of this 'second call.' She was absolutely sure that this was her vocation."

As Mother Teresa explained it, this was a "call within a call." She would remain a nun, and only her work would change.

A Complicated Process

She may have underestimated the process by which a Sister leaves her religious society and initiates another type of ministry. When she asked Father van Exem to bring the matter to the attention of Archbishop Perier of Calcutta, the priest was shocked by the prelate's reaction. He wondered how a European nun could engage in a ministry in the streets of the city at a time when political and social turmoil was the order of the day. Father van Exem attempted to explain that Mother Teresa's vision of her future work was the will of God, and that the Archbishop could not change the will of God!

The remark touched a raw archiepiscopal nerve, and Perier fairly shouted: "I am the archbishop, and I do not know the will of God. How can you, a young priest in Calcutta, know the will of God?"

Mother Teresa waited for a whole year. No word from the archbishop. At the end of 1947 he finally gave her permission to write to her own superior, the mother general of the Sisters of

Loreto at Rathfarman, to ask for the required approval to leave. When the archbishop saw her letter, he insisted that she request "secularization" that is, she would be working, not as a nun, but as an ordinary lay person. Both Mother Teresa and Father van Exem were shocked by the prelate's insistence. Bowing to his demands, however, the good Sister did as he dictated.

The reply from the mother general went through the archbishop's office, but his request for use of the word "secularization" was ignored. Wrote the mother general: "Dear Mother Teresa, Since this has been manifested as the will of God, I hereby give you permission to write to Rome. Do not speak to your local superior and do not speak to your provincial. My consent is sufficient. However, when you write to Rome, do not ask for 'secularization.' "

Mother Teresa had won her point. Both she and Father van Exem were jubilant. But the matter was not quite resolved yet. Archbishop Perier insisted once again on the use of the word "secularization" instead of "exclaustration" in her appeal to Rome. Dutifully, she reworded the letter and gave it to Father van Exem to present to the archbishop.

It wasn't until July 1948 that the decree from Rome reached the archbishop of Calcutta, granting Mother Teresa an Indult of Exclaustration. Armed with this official Vatican document, she could now begin her work in the slums at once. Her spiritual director suggested that she decide on what sort of habit she would wear. Teresa selected one that her followers still use today—a white "sari" with a blue border. Van Exem also cautioned her to delay her sidewalk apostolate until she acquired some medical training. He realized that teaching in a classroom was one thing, but coming face to face with diseased and dying people posed a different sort of problem.

Contact was made with the Medical Sisters in Patna, who invited Teresa to take some medical training in their hospital.

While receiving the equivalent of a para-medic's training, Mother Teresa realized that back in her home town of Skopje, her mother had no idea of what was happening. Even though she had written to her and told her that she might be leaving the Sisters of Loreto, she felt that Father van Exem should follow up with a longer letter of his own, detailing the permission received from Rome, her continuing status as a nun, and the nature of the work she would be doing. Father van Exem was pleased to do that favor for her.

A Step in Another Direction

On August 17, 1948, Mother Teresa proudly wore for the first time the white sari with the blue border that would in time serve as an identification for her followers the world over. On the night of August 17, she quietly left the convent at Entally where she had been living, and took the first steps of her "little way" in pursuit of her "second calling." No longer would she face classrooms with the children of the fairly well-to-do families of the city. Now the city itself would be her school, and her students would be the extremely poor, the homeless, the unloved, all those who had never found a place in society.

One can well imagine the thoughts that ran through her mind as she ventured out on her new mission. It was considerably difficult to leave the quiet and ordered way of convent life, separating herself from the Sisters with whom she had prayed and bonded herself in a spirit of sacrifice. Where would she find accommodations? Where would the funds come from to enable her to live and also care for the many needs of the poor she would befriend?

Mother Teresa was fortunate to enjoy the assistance and support of the Sisters of Loreto, who provided her with an undetermined amount of money, offered her chairs, tables, beds, and linens. Soon she was able to open a dispensary at St. Mary's School. Additionally, four Sisters of the Loreto community were allowed to join her "We gave her four of our very best," declared Sister Rozarion, superior of the convent at Entally.

Canonical Status

The general letter of approval which Mother Teresa received from Rome still required what is called "Canonical Approval." This consists of a very specific document that verifies the fact that Rome has given its full stamp of approval on a proposed new religious society. Saintly Pius XII was the reigning pope who signed the document on October 7, 1950. A simple ceremony celebrating this canonical endorsement was held at a convent at 14 Creek Lane, Calcutta. A small group of nuns gathered around Teresa to congratulate her and wish her well for the years and trials ahead.

Temporary Lodging

Until she could find a place to rent, Mother Teresa was a guest of the Little Sisters of the Poor who conducted a shelter where the homeless could find lodging. Every day she would leave there, taking with her a sandwich for lunch. Very often, however, she never had a chance to enjoy the sandwich because she would offer it to some hungry person lying in the street. After a long and tiring day of caring for the street people, she would return home, hungry and exhausted, and often without even a few rupees in her pocket. Like her sandwich, these too found their way into the hands of the needy.

In time, a Jesuit friend of hers, Father Michael Gomes, located a third-floor apartment that could be rented reasonably. A former student of Mother Teresa came to her and asked if she could join her. The good nun advised this postulant to think the matter over very seriously. "You will have to give up a great deal. I know your family is fairly well off, but you will be sharing the life of the poor. Pray over this matter, and I will pray for you as well."

A week later, the postulant, Sabashini Das, returned, fully determined to join Mother Teresa. She soon received her white sari with the blue border, her official habit in the new religious society. Others followed her example. The first ten were alumnae of the Sisters of Loreto schools in Calcutta. In a few years the number of Sisters grew to 28, and their quarters became far too small for them.

In October 1950 Rome extended the original one-year time frame for the work of Mother Teresa outside her former religious community. Based on the rapidly increasing number of young women associating themselves with Mother Teresa, Vatican officials approved the founding of the Missionaries of Charity. They were to work for the poorest of the poor. Mother Teresa's "second call" was being realized.

Archbishop Perier kept abreast of these events and became convinced that Mother Teresa's apostolic work was on solid footing. Through friends, he arranged for the purchase of a rather large building in Calcutta from a Muslim official. This building eventually became the headquarters of the Missionaries of Charity.

Mother Teresa with her Sisters and Archbishop Theodore McCarrick of Newark, New Jersey.
—Courtesy Archdiocese of Newark

3

Houses for the Dying

*Let us not make a mistake . . . the mistake of thinking
that hunger is only for a piece of bread. The hunger of
today is much greater: hunger for love, hunger to be
wanted, to be loved, to be cared for; to be somebody.*

—Mother Teresa

A tragic—and very familiar—scene in Calcutta
is the sight of people dying in the streets, in dark
alleys, on sidewalks, wherever these unfortunate
people collapse to await the inevitable hand of
death. The scene was so common that hardly
anyone paid attention to what had become a way
of life and death in India.

Teresa was appalled by the government's total
lack of concern for this situation and resolved to
do something about it. One day she found a
woman half eaten by rats, lying in the rain. The
compassionate nun gathered up the bleeding and
almost lifeless body and carried her to nearby
Campbell Hospital. Hospital personnel there cold-
ly told Teresa to take the woman back to the
streets and let her die there! Still hopeful of finding
medical help, the poor nun struggled to carry her
to other hospitals, only to hear the same words of
rejection. The unfortunate woman died in Mother

Teresa's arms. Teresa whispered a prayer over the woman's body and decided then and there to do something about this terrible situation.

Going to the Mayor of Calcutta, she described the shocking scenes she had witnessed time and time again, and requested some facility where her Sisters could care for these dying people. She was so insistent that the mayor could hardly deny her request. Two facilities were offered to her. The building she chose became known as the "House of the Dying."

There was considerable opposition to this gift from the municipality, but when one of those opposed to the idea became deathly ill and no hospital would accept him, he turned to Mother Teresa and her Sisters. They graciously admitted him and took excellent care of him.

In time, this hospital became the focal point of Mother Teresa's work, and civic authorities placed it on the "must see" attractions in Calcutta. Someone remarked that to bypass this hospital on a visit to Calcutta would be like going to Rome and neglecting to visit the Vatican. Not long after its opening, the hospital started to attract medical students who found it an ideal setting for their work. Some students gave up their weeks of vacation to work there under the guidance of Mother Teresa and her Sisters.

Volunteers also flocked there from other walks of life, deeply impressed by the quality of the care extended to the dying and the obvious dedication of Mother Teresa. Some of these women requested membership in the Missionaries of Charity. After professing their vows, they continued to work at the Hospital for the Dying, or at other facilities founded by Mother Teresa.

A characteristic of the Hospital for the Dying was its openness to people of any religious faith or no faith at all. Everyone appreciated the warm welcome given them by Mother Teresa and her associates. No one felt out of place or unloved.

While Mother Teresa was never overly concerned with statistics—she felt that record-keeping used up valuable time—she did announce that approximately 2,000 citizens of Calcutta had passed on to eternity while sharing the warmth and care of her Sisters. With reference to this, she once remarked: "Of all those who died here, I never saw even one who died in desperation. When they were at the point of death, the Sisters simply asked them: "Would you like to have a blessing to obtain from God forgiveness of your sins and be able to enjoy His presence forever?"

No one ever refused this blessing. And among the Sisters the usual conversation piece was: "Did you give them a ticket for St. Peter?"

Gradual Development

As new hospitals, clinics, refuge centers, and facilities for the dying brought Mother Teresa's compassionate ministry for the poorest of the poor to many different cities and countries, Teresa repeatedly stated: "We have no specific plans when we begin a new operation; we go where we feel God is calling us. We look for the poorest of the poor, abandoned children, the dying, the homeless, and the abandoned. It has been God who shows us the way."

Although Mother Teresa was always deeply involved in her ministry, she never lost sight of her desire to become a saint, and to encourage her Sisters to do likewise. She once said: "If in spite of so many difficulties we can still work with all our heart for the poor, we remain on the road that leads to sanctity."

Concern for God's Little Ones

While committed to the care of the dying in her hospitals, Mother Teresa never lost sight of the poor children who were often left homeless and abandoned by their parents. On many occasions she found little children hovering over the bodies of their dead mothers and fathers. Several facilities for the young were entrusted to the Missionaries of Charity, such as the one given by

the Imperial Chemical Industries, and one by the
Kennedy Family. In some cities, such as Rome
and Florence, the Sisters conduct shelters for
both little children and their mothers. In some
cases, the mothers are extremely young; in other
cases, wives are abandoned by their husbands,
or have serious personal problems.

Love for the Poor

Mother Teresa often said: "The poor are wonderful." For her, this expression was not mere
rhetoric or pious fluff to win sympathy for her
work. She truly believed it. It reflected the deep
love in her heart for God's "poorest of the poor."
She came in contact with large numbers of them
daily and realized what it meant for them to be
homeless, hungry, with no one to love them or
care for them. She had seen them half-naked,
lying in the streets of Calcutta, with people pass-
ing them by without so much as giving them a
glance or a glass of water. She saw them sleeping
in dark alleys, covered with paper and straw and
rags. In spite of all that, she considered the poor
"wonderful people."

One day Mother Teresa was told that a mother and her many children had not eaten for some
time. She quickly prepared some rice and bread

and rushed to bring the food to this unfortunate family. The hungry mother distributed half of the food among her children, and put the remainder aside. Mother Teresa asked what she would do with it. The woman replied: "There is another mother nearby with many children, and I will bring them what I did not eat." Mother Teresa learned later that one of the families was Muslim, the other Buddhist.

She used to tell the story of a young child who was dying of hunger, but took the food that was given to her by Mother Teresa's Sisters to her even hungrier father, who was sick. Another of Mother's stories was of a poor old man who kept his dead wife alongside him while he begged for alms to buy her a casket!

Care of Lepers

Leprosy is a very ancient disease. We read about it in both the Old and the New Testament. The Book of Leviticus tells us: "Lepers shall live outside their communities. They shall go about shouting "Unclean! Unclean."

India has always had an abundance of lepers. who were shunned by the general public and received little or no care from civic officials. From the very beginning of her work, Mother Teresa had a soft spot in her heart for lepers.

There are approximately thirteen million lepers in the world. Of these, about four million live in India. Mother Teresa had ample opportunity to come in contact with them in Calcutta and other areas of India. By law, their ties with their families and with society in general are cut off, and they are forced to live in isolation.

In her concern for lepers, Mother Teresa founded hospitals and villages dedicated to their care. In India alone the Missionaries of Charity operate approximately eighty hospitals for lepers. This work began in 1957 with five lepers. When she began her work for these unfortunate people, Mother Teresa traveled around the city in an ambulance, looking for them where they could usually be found. At first she provided them with medicine. Later she organized hospitals and clinics devoted solely to lepers.

Her first village for lepers, called Shantinagha (Place of Peace), was located about 25 miles outside Calcutta. Here the lepers could live with a little more dignity in clean quarters and with caring attention by the Sisters and their medical collaborators. The village was built on 24 acres donated by the government of Bengal. Funding for the buildings came from several nations. It was dedicated on the Feast of St. Joseph, March 19, 1974.

Titagarh, an area several miles outside Calcutta, is the site of another colony of lepers cared for by Mother Teresa's followers. It is called "Ghanhiji's Prem Nivas," meaning "The Gift of Love of Mahatama Gandhi." Today this refuge caters to the lepers' many needs. In addition to medical help, they also find this place an uplifting setting for the recovery of their faith if they have lost it. Among its many facilities are a hospital, clinics, sleeping quarters, laboratories, private homes for small families and a reservoir for water for the entire community.

The Brother Missionaries of Charity also work here and provide opportunities for employment for the lepers. The Brothers assist the many doctors who volunteer their services for the lepers, some, one day every week.

4

Travels Abroad

Let us remember that the good things we do are only like a drop of water in the ocean, but without that drop of water, the ocean would be smaller. —Mother Teresa

In the fall of 1960 Mother Teresa made her first visits to Italy, the United States, England, Germany and Switzerland. Wherever she went, her presence generated enthusiasm for her work in India. People went out of their way to offer financial help or to join her Sisters. While not interested in organizing formal "cooperators" among the laity, as so many religious societies have done, Mother Teresa did encourage those who wanted to help to make their informal partnership with the Sisters a way of sanctifying themselves. She made it very clear that the sanctification of these volunteers was her primary concern.

New York was among the earlier mission sites she established after branching out internationally in 1967 from her original foundation in Calcutta. The New York mission has expanded in the metropolitan area to include two convents in the Bronx and one in Harlem. There is a residence in Manhattan for homeless AIDS patients, and houses in Brooklyn and Newark, New Jersey.

One of the convents in the Bronx is contemplative, where the Sisters spend much of their time in prayer and meditation. The Harlem convent provides a soup kitchen and a women's shelter.

Brother Missionaries of Charity

As often happens when a religious society of men or women is begun, a companion society is founded by the opposite gender. In 1859 John Bosco founded the Salesian Fathers and Brothers, whose work was primarily focused on boys of elementary and secondary school age. Later, with Saint Mary Mazzarello, he co-founded the Salesian Sisters (Daughters of Mary Help of Christians). Similar developments took place with the Franciscans, the Carmelites, and others.

By 1960 the need for male religious to extend the work of Mother Teresa's Sisters became quite apparent. Mother Teresa already had some male associates working with her and many others were interested in joining this group. While she could find no one who was interested in serving as a co-founder, she eventually (1963) heard of a small group of men working for the poor in the same spirit of Mother Teresa. The Jesuit founder, Father Ian Travers-Ball, had heard a talk given by Mother Teresa shortly before he took his solemn vows. He was so impressed with her fervor and evangelical spirit that he resolved to work with her.

When they met, Teresa asked the young priest: "Father, would you be willing to take care of these young men that are working with me, and monitor their spiritual formation? He took some time to reflect on her invitation and to consult his religious superiors who offered him several choices. He could work with Mother Teresa for two years, while still remaining a member of the Society of Jesus, or he could be dispensed from his vows and join her Brothers of Charity. He chose to become a Brother of Charity and assume leadership of the group. His name was changed to Brother Andrew, and he brought with him his intense training as a Jesuit, his spirit of optimism, and his willingness to be of service to the Brothers of Charity.

The results of his involvement in the work of the Brothers of Charity became evident in a short time. Their numbers increased dramatically, and soon some of them went off to missionary work in America, Africa, France, Switzerland and Finland. Father Travers-Ball continued as head of the Brothers until 1988.

Worldwide Expansion

Mother Teresa's Missionaries of Charity experienced phenomenal growth over the years.

Foundations were begun in England, Italy, Germany, France, Peru, Panama, Austria, Portugal, Poland, Hungary, Romania, Czechoslovakia, Brazil and Australia. Foundations in the United States have already been mentioned.

In 1976 Mother Teresa was invited by Cardinal Taracon of Madrid to bring her Missionaries of Charity to work in a suburb of the city. In keeping with the routine for considering such invitations, Mother Teresa wanted to "check out" the area in question.

Arriving at the airport Mother Teresa's Indian passport was not enough to allow her to enter into Spain. A visa was also needed. The stewardess pressed her point, stressing the worldwide renown of the person in question. The police agreed to appeal to their superior. In the meantime, Mother Teresa took out her Vatican passport, which is one of the most powerful in the world. On seeing it, the airport official exclaimed: "My God, if you had presented that before, all doors would have been opened to you without the need for any delay and further permission from anyone."

Mother Teresa's evangelical mission that began so humbly on October 7, 1950, is now flourishing all over the world, thanks to the indefatigable spirit of this great soul. By May 1992, her sisters, brothers, and priest missionaries were at work in ninety-seven countries on five continents. Their "collaborators" were also at work in seventy countries.

"I often remind my followers," said Mother Teresa, "that during the three years of his public life, Jesus dedicated himself to the sick, the lepers, and children. We are doing the same thing, as we preach his Gospel by our actions. It is a privilege for us to serve God's people, working for them with all our heart. What we do may be like a drop of water in the ocean, but without that drop, the ocean would be smaller."

Human Touches

Once, when Mother Teresa was spending a few days in a European city, she was surprised that there were so few children around. While walking through the city, she spotted a baby carriage being pushed by a young woman on the sidewalk on the opposite side of the street. She crossed the street to look at the baby and chat with the young mother. When she came close to the baby carriage, to her astonishment she noticed there was no baby in the carriage. There was a little puppy!

In another city she and a few other Sisters were living in a house rented from a neighbor, who had a puppy named Timmy. All the Sisters took to the puppy, and spent time with him every now and then, petting him, teasing him, and generally displaying great love for the puppy. Some time later the Sisters had to move to another section of the city to be closer to homeless people. It was with genuine reluctance that they parted company with the puppy. Friends later told them that Timmy missed them so much that he took off one day and did not return.

Every Day Miracles

People marveled at the fact that in so many cities where the Sisters ran their soup kitchens for the poorest of the poor, they never ran out of food. Day after day hundreds of hungry and abandoned people came to accept whatever the Sisters had to offer them. Never did they have to turn anyone away. The food simply came right on coming. Dishes were always full. Now and them some stragglers would arrive and ask if there was any food left for them. The Sisters would gently chide them and remind them that they had to be on time. Then they would call the Sisters in the kitchen and ask if anything was left. Without fail, there always was!

5

Gifts from Many Sources

We must do small things for one another with love.

Is it possible to involve oneself in an apostolate without having a spirit of prayer? —Mother Teresa

An interesting feature of the life of the Missionaries of Charity was their total independence from government help in their work. Mother Teresa made it one of their treasured norms: no dependence on fixed income from the government or other sources. Charitable donations from many sources were always welcome, but it had to be understood that these were goodwill offerings and nothing else.

Mother Teresa loved to tell the story of her meeting with Terence Cardinal Cooke in New York. He suggested that a fixed amount of money be earmarked for the Sisters every month. Struggling to find words to refuse his gracious offer, Mother Teresa told the cardinal: "Your Eminence, God has taken care of us everywhere, even in the poorest countries. Do you think He will let us down here in New York? I thank you from the bottom of my heart, your Eminence, but please don't worry about us."

She recorded another similar story. A bishop in Belgium wrote to her and assured her he could provide a very beautiful house for the Sisters and give each one the equivalent of 250 rupees every week—a most attractive offer given in genuine concern. "I answered his letter," commented Mother Teresa, "and told him that I thanked him very sincerely, but we only accept unfortunate people, those suffering from lack of homes and food and clothing."

As word of Mother Teresa's charitable programs for the poorest of the poor circulated throughout the world, people from many walks of life presented her with a variety of gifts: jewels, money, buildings, and land. One Saturday morning an elderly gentleman came to visit Mother Teresa. He said that he found great difficulty in tracking down her residence in Calcutta because he came from a distant land. She greeted him very warmly and asked how she could help him.

"I didn't come here for help, Sister. I came to bring you jewels, a ring, and bracelets that belonged to my wife. She passed away a few weeks ago and had always told me that she wanted her jewelry to be given to you and your Missionaries of Charity for the wonderful work you are doing for God's poorest creatures. All I ask in return are your prayers for my wife and myself. We had no children. We want no thanks or public recognition."

Mother Teresa thanked him profusely as he handed over the jewelry. Then he said he would have to start back to his home—in Spain! He retrieved his cane and left.

Public Thanks

Sisters who worked with Mother Teresa soon learned how precise and conscientious she was in recording and honoring the gifts she received, no matter how small. The intentions of the donors always had to be respected. If money were given to fights AIDS, it could only be used for that purpose. She was equally insistent with her Sisters that they appreciate the value of all signs of respect and courtesy.

Speaking of gifts, Mother Teresa always maintained that it was not how much we give, but the intensity of love with which we give. In some cases she expressed her gratitude publicly when she felt the donors could provide good examples by their generosity. She did this with Imperial Chemical Industries, a company that offered her a building and land, which enabled her to provide an excellent facility for children with serious handicaps and physical problems. She called that clinic "The Gift of Hope."

After she had been honored with the Nobel Peace Prize and substantial financial awards, she met a beggar in Calcutta, who told her: "Mother Teresa, I see that you have been honored by many people. I want to make my little offering. Here is the money I received today from my begging."

She was deeply moved by his kindness, and told him she appreciated his generosity even more than the funds received from the Nobel Peace Prize. She, like Christ in the temple, was touched by the gift of a very poor person. "We should give not only from our abundance, but also to the point where it hurts," was her belief.

Countless Friends

Everyone loves to have friends with whom to share life's many blessings. It may be no exaggeration to claim that Mother Teresa had more friends than most other people. They came from all walks of life: from the ranks of clergy, Sisters, distinguished writers, royalty (King Baudovin and Queen Sofia of Spain), Indira Gandhi, statesmen, political leaders, university professors, and ordinary people. Some of them were wealthy, others poor or struggling. Everyone was thrilled to see and meet Mother Teresa. She made everyone feel as if he or she were the most important person in the world. Father Benedict Groeschel, C.F.R., director of the New York Archdiocese Office of Spiritual Development, gives his reaction to his first meeting with Mother Teresa: "It was the oddest experience. I forgot all the people in the room. It was like standing there and talking to her in the middle of an empty field. When you talked to her, you had her attention."

John Cardinal O'Connor of New York observed: "What made her special was the way she looked at people, talked with people, as though this individual was the only person in the world."

Photographers followed her wherever she went. She patiently endured the flashes of their cameras, and once said: "I pray to God that every flash would free a soul from purgatory."

Approval of Collaborators

When Pope Paul VI on March 26, 1969, approved the status of her International Association of Collaborators, he asked Mother Teresa to consider him a humble collaborator with her work. And when she requested approval of Priest Collaborators, he again asked her to include him in that organization. "List me," he urged, "as one of the very first to join the group of Priest Collaborators."

With reference to the growing number of collaborators (people from all walks of life who share their time and talent with the Sisters), Mother Teresa insisted that she was not concerned with rules and regulations, but with the intensity of the love with which people worked and their willingness to work harmoniously with others.

© Servizio Fotograpico de "L'O.R.", 00120 Citta del Vaticano

"We must be prepared to see, love, and serve Christ in the poorest of the poor." She always had great respect for the non-Catholics among her collaborators. Love for Christ and His poor people was the only yardstick for accepting these good people into her organizations.

Variety of Opportunities

Mother Teresa and her Sisters cataloged a list of areas where people could be of help: peeling potatoes, serving at table, cleaning the sidewalks, cutting fingernails and toenails for the poor, shaving them and giving them haircuts, washing the sick in the clinics, visiting the elderly, carrying articles of clothing to places where they were needed, cleaning the homes of the handicapped and the elderly, and accompanying people on walks. The Sisters assigned the volunteers to those areas where they felt most able and would enjoy doing that type of work.

Mother Teresa also found collaborators among various airlines, particularly Air India, Alitalia, Pan American, British Airways, and Air France. They often provided her and her Sisters with free tickets. Once, when she was given six passes, she sent six Sisters with an enormous amount of "baggage"—blankets, medical supplies, linens, clothing, etc. Her reasoning was: the passes simply read "For six Sisters and their respective baggage." Counter personnel were amazed when they saw the six Sisters and the supplies they were taking along. No one said a word, and the Sisters arrived safely at their destination, almost fully equipped to start up another clinic!

Airline personnel helped in other ways as well. One flight attendant on a Boeing jumbo jet usually had a few "stand-bys" on her flights to European capitals. She spent that time helping at one of Mother Teresa's clinics or hospitals. One pilot on a major airline, a great friend of Mother Teresa, often visited her foundations in several countries and spent time assisting the Sisters in various ways. Other attendants took care of babies up for adoption in distant countries.

All of this outpouring of volunteer help was the result of the personal magnetism of Mother Teresa and the enthusiasm for her ministry which she generated easily.

Jesuit Relationships

Brother Andrew, the former Jesuit, who was a co-founder with Mother Teresa of the Brother Missionaries of Charity often spoke of the mischievous smile on her face when she referred to her "snatching of Brother Andrew from the Jesuits." This was no mean achievement. Sharing with Mother Teresa in her compassionate work for the poorest of the poor was his great delight. He made no secret of the fact that while training young men for the Brother Missionaries of Charity, he managed to include some Ignatian principles in their lifestyle!

Occasionally, Mother Teresa frowned on some of the changes he introduced, but she respected his work and had great confidence in him. "Her spirit of cooperation always made me feel very comfortable," Brother Andrew remarked.

Brother Andrew continued to serve as head of the Congregation of Missionary Brothers for twenty years. During this time he provided spiritual leadership and guidance for the Brothers. In 1988 he decided to give up the leadership of the group, and he returned to Australia where he dedicated himself to preaching the Spiritual Exercises of Saint Ignatius. In 1991 he returned to Calcutta and met with Mother Teresa for the last time.

Commenting on this meeting, he writes: "I found Mother Teresa looking somewhat old. She had been ill, and her voice was very weak. But to hear her describe some of the developments of the Missionaries of Charity, you sensed you were speaking with an extraordinary woman. She spoke glowingly of the seven new communities of her Sisters in Russia, of the five young Albanians who were joining the Society, and about candidates from Romania and Hungary. In the past few weeks she had opened seven communities in Cuba and maintained contacts with Fidel Castro. Recently, too, at the invitation of Saddam Hussein, she had been in Iraq, where the Missionaries of Charity were taking care of orphans of the war, many of them severely injured."

Selecting Names

It is interesting that Mother Teresa and her Sisters chose some rather unusual names for their clinics, hospitals and refuges. There are such names as "Star of the Morning," "Gift of Peace," "House of Peace," "Queen of Peace," "House of Happiness," and "House, Gift of Mary."

This policy is in contrast to the practices of many religious societies which use the names of their founders or former heads of the congregations. For example, the Salesian Fathers and Brothers of Don Bosco, Eastern Province, USA, have many schools in the same general area with the name of the founder: Don Bosco College, Don Bosco Seminary, Don Bosco Preparatory High School, Don Bosco Technical High School. The Missionaries of Charity on the other hand, feel it is more important to draw attention to their work than their founder.

6

Leading Ministries

It's Christmas time every time you smile at someone. It's Christmas time every time you stop to listen to someone. It's Christmas time every time you allow Jesus to love someone through you. —Mother Teresa

As we examine the work of the Missionaries of Charity around the world, we find Mother Teresa's Sisters engaged in the following ministries:

1) apostolic work in schools through catechetical instruction, Catholic Action groups, visits to those in prisons and in hospitals

2) medical assistance in dispensaries, clinics (some mobile), leprosaria, hospitals, homes for abandoned children, the sick, the dying, and victims of AIDS

3) educational services in elementary schools, pre-school and after-school activities

4) social service programs for single mothers, the homeless, those dependent on narcotics, etc.

5) support services by way of food distribution facilities and countless outreach programs to poor families

At times very unusual things happened with reference to these programs. Once, when Mother

Teresa was in London, she received a phone call from the police. "Mother Teresa, there is a lady here, quite beastly inebriated. She wants you, and will not move until you come."

Mother Teresa, with another Sister, went at once. While they were approaching the woman and the police, she cried out: "Mother Teresa, is it true that Jesus is good? He changed water into wine so that we could have something to drink!" With an understanding smile, Mother Teresa embraced her and took her to one of her centers where the poor woman found hospitality and friendship.

Further Growth

In 1965, the year Pope Paul VI gave her society pontifical approval, Mother Teresa's Sisters were able to extend their work worldwide. On July 25, 1965, Mother Teresa and two Sisters opened a house for the very needy in Cocorote, Venezuela. In short order, they founded other centers in Peru, Colombia, Brazil, Argentina, Guatemala, and Uraguay. In every instance, they focused their attention on the neediest.

Central America and the Caribbean were the next beneficiaries of their work, with hospitals and clinics in Cuba, the Dominican Republic, El Salvador, Grenada, Haiti, Honduras and Puerto Rico.

In 1971 Mother Teresa and her Sisters set foot in the Mid-East. Today they are busily at work in Palestine, Israel, Jordan, Lebanon, Syria and Yemen, where for eight centuries no priests or religious had ever been.

Toward the end of the 1980s, in India alone, the Missionaries of Charity were at work in practically every diocese, offering their services in 543 foundations. Additionally, there were in India 46 communities of the Brother Missionaries of Charity and two communities of Contemplative Missionaries.

As of 1999, they can be found in thirty communities in the United States and several in Canada. In Africa, their ministry caters to the poorest of the poor in such places as Benin, Burundi, Ethiopia, Ghana, Kenya, Madagascar, Sudan, Nigeria, Tanzania, and Egypt.

Eileen Egan, a very active collaborator with Mother Teresa, recalls that one day Mother gathered a group of Sisters around her. On the wall was a large map with little flags indicating where the Missionaries of Charity were at work in India, Asia, Australia, the Middle East, Africa, South America and North America. "All these foundations," said Mother Teresa," are places that God has made from nothing. People must understand that this is all God's work. We must allow God to use us." These words of Mother Teresa reflect her profound conviction that God was truly at work through the Sisters.

In addition to many foundations in India, her Sisters have houses in Bangladesh, Hong Kong, Japan, South Korea, Macao, Nepal, Pakistan, the Philippines, Singapore, Sri Lanka, Taiwan and Vietnam. In 1996 they opened a center in Beijing, China.

When her Sisters were invited to open a clinic in Yemen, Mother Teresa requested the right to take along a priest for Mass and the sacraments. The government granted this request, and Mother Teresa exclaimed, "Finally, Christ has returned to His people."

After the Gulf War, Saddam Hussein invited Mother Teresa and her Sisters to work in Iraq. With the help of many friends they were able to open a residence for little children, providing them with food, clothing, suitable accommodations, and sincere love and care. The government of Iraq also gave the Sisters a truck which they transformed into a mobile clinic.

Nirmala Shishu Bavan

One of the largest complexes that Mother Teresa built over the years was in Calcutta not far from her motherhouse or general headquarters in Nirmala Shishu Bavan. It is a sprawling series of buildings with each section catering to the special needs of various segments of God's "poorest of the poor."

One building has a large emergency room where injured people can receive prompt attention. Nearby is a gathering place for newly-born babies who have been abandoned. A twenty-four-hour pharmacy provides medication and medical supplies. A section of another building provides personnel to help interested parties to fill out forms for adoption.

Actually, it is like a small village that simply kept on growing to meet the needs of the thousands who came for help.

One has to be amazed by the work Mother Teresa has done to offer as much help as possible to poor people in every stage of life: the elderly, the homeless, the abandoned, the uncared for, the sick and neglected, those left to die in the streets, victims of domestic violence, the outcasts of society, and those who have fallen through the cracks of society.

7

European Foundations

When I give food to a child, I am giving food to Christ.
When I touch a leper, I am touching Christ. Let us give
medicine as if we were giving Communion.

—Mother Teresa

In Europe the Missionaries of Charity conduct more than one hundred foundations in: Finland, Lithuania, Estonia, Russia, Poland, Austria, Germany, Holland, Belgium, France, Portugal, Spain, Great Britain, Ireland, Greece, Romania, Hungary, the Czech Republic, Albania, and Italy.

Statistics of the foundations change quickly, because her congregation is constantly responding to requests of bishops and governments all over the world.

First House in Rome

It has been said many times that wherever there are the poor, there is Mother Teresa of Calcutta. She reminded her Sisters many times: "We do everything for Jesus. Jesus is the Love that has to be loved. He is the Joy that has to be shared. He is the hungry one who has to be nourished. He is the sick one who has to be healed. He is the lonely person who has to be consoled. Jesus is our everything."

At the request of Pope Paul VI she opened her first foundation in Rome in 1968. She realized that even Rome had its very poor and its homeless, and on May 21, 1988, she realized one of her fondest dreams—to have a clinic in the Vatican. She called it "The Gift of Mary." It was offered to her by the pope himself. Commenting on this special request, she said: "The pope has given us a gift, a section of his own house, where we can receive and take care of the sick and the poor. These poor people are Jesus. And how could we leave Jesus, sad and cold, outside the house of the pope himself?"

Pope's Visit - 1986

During his 1986 visit to India, Pope John Paul II spent considerable time with Mother Teresa. She took him on a tour of Nirmal Hriday, her world-renowned hospital for the dying. Greatly impressed by what he saw, the pope said it was not only a place for those who suffer, but also a place of hope, a house where love reigns supreme, a place of faith and courage. "This place proclaims the profound dignity of every human being. No suffering can diminish this dignity because we are always precious in the sight of God."

"It was the happiest day of my life," declared Mother Teresa. The pope's kind words and his appreciation for the work that she and her Sisters were doing gave courage and confidence to everyone.

She recalled how once, while walking through the streets of Calcutta, she came across something that was moving. Only when she came closer did she realize it was a human being covered with sores and dirt, hardly distinguishable as a person. As Mother Teresa picked him up and carried him to her house for the dying, she heard a weak voice say: "I have lived all my life like an animal on the street. Now I will die as an angel, surrounded by love and attention."

Later Mother Teresa commented, "It took us three hours to clean that poor body. That body was the body of Christ." After his body had been cleaned by the Sisters, the man looked up at those around him and said, "Sisters, I am returning to the house of God." Mother Teresa could never forget the smile on the dying man's face. "There was not the slightest sign of despair. You could sense his complete abandonment to the will of God."

Honorary Citizen of Rome

On May 1, 1996, Mayor Francis Rutelli of Rome decided to make Mother Teresa an honorary citizen. He considered her one of the most beloved women in the world. Her Missionaries of Charity were hard at work in several houses in Rome where they cared for the poor, AIDS victims, very young mothers and the elderly.

"All the world recognizes Mother Teresa as a spiritual guide, said Rutelli, a woman of great strength who has inspired both Christians and non-Christians to great acts of kindness."

The mayor also reminded his fellow citizens that Mother Teresa had been instrumental in arranging for the adoption of children for thousands of families in Rome.

Visit to Moscow

In August, 1987, she was invited to Moscow by the Soviet Committee for Peace.

They wanted her to see the place where some survivors of the nuclear blast in Chernobyl were living. Mother spoke of her meeting with the committee members as very friendly. One committee member told her: "You speak of God; we speak of nature, and maybe they are the same thing." They presented her with a bouquet of flowers and a gold medal. Some people wondered whether Mother Teresa had come to Moscow to seek permission for her Sisters to open a foundation in Russia. This did not happen until after the earthquake in Armenia in

December 1988. One of the first ones to offer assistance to the survivors was Mother Teresa.

"I have neither silver nor gold," she said, "but I hope to bring my volunteers to help with the work of caring for those injured." A few days later, the official Russian news agency carried this notice: "The Missionaries of Charity of Mother Teresa have received permission to work in the Soviet Union for the elderly, the homeless, and the injured. This is the first time since the Russian Revolution that a foreign organization has been authorized to establish itself in the Soviet Union."

This surprising piece of information was published at about the same time that Mother Teresa was admitted to St. Vincent's Hospital in New York for a cataract operation. The successful surgery took place just a few days after she had returned from Cuba, where she had opened two new houses for her Sisters. It was difficult indeed for people to keep track of this globe-trotting nun—Russia, Cuba, New York, Rome, India. She did God's work everywhere.

On to Romania

On May 2, 1990, Mother Teresa opened her first house in Romania to tend to the needs of AIDS victims and in March 1991, she went to

Albania, the land of her birth. In spite of the atheistic government that had dominated the country for many years, she was granted permission to open a center for her fellow Albanians. A short time later she opened a welcoming center for the poor and sick in Tirana, and later in Scutari. She also obtained permission to reopen the Church of Saint Anthony and the Cathedral of the Sacred Heart. In a modest sort of way, this was indeed a triumphant return home for the young postulant who had left for Ireland to become a member of the Sisters of Loreto in 1928.

She arranged for baptisms, and was delighted to see the crucifix begin to regain its place in many homes. At this time, too, she was able to visit her mother's grave in the cemetery in Kombinat on the outskirts of Tirana. She prayed fervently at her dear mother's final resting place on earth. Mother Teresa had not seen her mother from the time she left home 63 years earlier to begin her studies in Ireland on October 13, 1928!

— 8 —

Champion for Life

We have fear of nuclear war; we have fear of this latest, terrible malady—AIDS. But we have no fear of killing an innocent baby. I believe that today abortion is the greatest destroyer of peace. —Mother Teresa

Again and again throughout her life Mother Teresa spoke out courageously against abortion. On March 1, 1979, when the President of Italy presented her with the Balzan Award, she used her acceptance speech to state clearly: "We want every baby, whether desired or not, to come into our world. Abortion is a crime. We are born to do great things. We are not just numbers."

Soon after, on the occasion of the presentation of the Nobel Peace Prize, her words of condemnation of abortion left no one unsure of her position. "The greatest enemy of peace is abortion—the crime against unborn babies."

At a speech before the United Nations in New York on October 26, 1983, Mother Teresa addressed the General Assembly and reminded that august assemblage that "When we destroy an embryo in the womb of a mother, we strike directly against God. We fear nuclear war, but we show not the slightest unease when we kill a baby in the mother's womb. Abortion has become the greatest threat against peace."

And in 1990, when Russia conferred the Tolstoy International Medal upon her, the presenter stated: "This award is made in recognition of the work, the courage, and the resolute stand which have distinguished Mother Teresa's defense of infants the world over."

"Leprosy of the West"

Mother Teresa refers to AIDS as the "leprosy of the West." Along with her worldwide work for society's outcasts and those who fell through the cracks, she exhibited a deep concern for victims of AIDS. In December of 1985, she opened a center for them in New York. Initial accommodations were for fifteen patients, but the number has risen steadily over the years. As in her other clinics and hospitals, Mother Teresa set aside one room as a chapel. She appreciated the therapeutic value of prayer and meditation for the patients and their caretakers.

The New York clinic was her first center for AIDS victims. A short time later, at the personal request of President Ronald Reagan, she opened a second house in Washington, D.C., called "The Gift of Peace." Similar clinics, geared to meet the

needs primarily of AIDS patients, were founded
by "God's Angel" in other parts of the world.

No longer simply "the leprosy of the West, AIDS
has spread astronomically in countless countries.
The World Health Organization estimates that
more than 33 million people in the world are
infected with the HIV virus. Statistically, the most
infected continent is Africa, with 22 million victims. Ignorance, lack of sanitary living conditions,
and outright disregard for the evil of AIDS account
for this phenomenal figure.

At the United Nations

On October 26, 1985, Mother Teresa was introduced to the United Nations General Assembly.
She was dressed in her usual white sari, bor-
dered in blue, with a small crucifix near her right
shoulder, her rosary beads in her hands, and her
feet in sandals. When Xavier Perez de Cuellar,
the U.N. Secretary General, introduced her, his
words were simple and stunning: "I present to
you the most powerful woman in the world." He
also brought a message from President Reagan
of the United States: "The whole world knows
the radiant style of this marvelous Christian
woman."

The Prime Minister of India paid great tribute
to her when he said: "We are very proud that

Mother Teresa adopted India as her own country. However, she belongs not to India alone, but to the whole world."

When Mother Teresa had been invited to speak after she was presented with the Nobel Peace Prize, she invited everyone to join her in a prayer. What more appropriate prayer for the occasion than the Prayer for Peace of St. Francis of Assisi?

> *Lord, make me an instrument of your peace:*
> *where there is hatred, let me sow love;*
> *where there is injury, pardon;*
> *where there is doubt, faith;*
> *where there is despair, hope;*
> *where there is darkness, light;*
> *and where there is sadness, joy.*
> *O Divine Master, grant that I might not so*
> *much seek*
> *to be consoled as to console,*
> *to be understood as to understand,*
> *to be loved as to love.*
> *For it is in giving that we receive,*
> *it is in pardoning that we are pardoned,*
> *and it is in dying that we are born to eternal*
> *life.*

In her speech to the General Assembly, Mother Teresa made this exhortation along with her denunciation of abortion: "We are united here today in thanking God on the occasion of the fortieth anniversary of the work of the United Nations on behalf of all mankind. Color, religion, and nationality cannot divide us. We are all children of God. We pray for peace here in this hall where nations meet one another to talk about peace."

Let's Do Something Beautiful for God

I am a pencil in the hands of God. He writes what He wills.

The fruit of silence is prayer; the fruit of prayer is faith; the fruit of faith is love; the fruit of love is service, and the fruit of service is peace. —Mother Teresa

Without fear of exaggerating, it can safely be said that no nun in the history of the Church was ever so exposed to the mass media as was Mother Teresa of Calcutta. A naturally shy and humble person, she had no choice but to accept the countless invitations to appear in public. To a great extent her work depended on it. How could she dismiss the TV cameras and journalists when she was being honored with the Nobel Peace Prize? How could she fail to show up in Moscow to receive the Medal of Peace in recognition for the work she was doing to promote peace? How could she have avoided being named "The Woman of the Year" by the government of India in December 1989?

Awards and honors

1962 "Magnificent Lotus", by the Government of India. Magsayeay Award for International Understanding, by the Philippines

1971 Pope John XXIII Peace Prize, by Pope Paul VI
Good Samaritan Award, by the USA
John F. Kennedy International Award, by the USA

1972 Jawaharlal Nehru Award for International Understanding, by the Government of India

1973 Templeton Award for Progress in Religion, by Great Britain

1974 "Mater et Magistra" Award, by the Third Order of St. Francis, USA

1975 FAO Ceres Medal, by the Italian Government
Albert Schweitzer Prize, by the USA
Twenty-fifth Anniversary Jubilee of the Missionaries of Charity, in India, with honors from 18 religious denominations

1976 Honorary Doctorate, Santiniketan, India

1977 Honorary Doctor of Divinity, Cambridge University

1979 Balzan International Prize, Rome
Honorary Doctorate, Temple University, USA
Nobel Peace Prize, Oslo

1980 Bharat Rathna, Government of India (Jewel of India)

1985 Presidential Medal of Freedom, USA

1989 Woman of the Year, India

1997 Congressional Gold Medal, US Congress

In addition to these major honors and awards, Mother Teresa received many other citations for her dedicated work. Probably the only reason that she accepted them was the fact that they included substantial donations. All of this financial assistance was immediately earmarked for the charitable work of her Sisters.

The magnitude of her apostolic work and the countless demands for the presence of her Sisters in just about every country in the world testify to the charismatic nature of her discipleship of Christ. It remains now for the Catholic Church to bestow on her the honors of the altar—sainthood. People the world over pressured Pope John Paul II to waive the five-year waiting period before the process leading to canonization can begin. He originally indicated that the usual time line would be followed, but he underestimated the immense pressure that would fall upon him after her death.

On March 13, 1997, the Missionaries of Charity elected Sister Nirmala as successor to Mother

Teresa. It was evident to everyone that Mother's health was rapidly deteriorating, and she could no longer carry the heavy burden of governing her worldwide organization.

In the months following the election, Mother Teresa spent many weeks with Sister Nirmala, reviewing the extensive network of hospitals, clinics, leprosaria, and other institutions where the Missionaries of Charity were carrying on their mission of mercy for the poor and the homeless.

One of Mother's remaining duties was to accompany the new superior general to the Vatican and present her to the pope. On her way back to India, she decided to stop in New York. John Cardinal O'Connor remarked, "She has an affinity for New York, and the people love her."

— 10 —

Death for God's Angel

Let us leave for the future every project we have in mind. Yesterday is gone; tomorrow has not yet come. We have only today to know, love and serve.

—Mother Teresa

Exhausted by her traveling, Mother Teresa attended Holy Mass on Friday, September 5, 1997. Not feeling well, she retired to her room, monitored by her Sisters, who realized that she was in serious condition. She had been hospitalized several times the preceding year for heart, lung, kidney and other ailments. Her physician, Vincenzo Bilotta, announced that Mother Teresa died of cardiac arrest during the evening of September 5 in her convent in Calcutta. She was 87. Her last words were "Jesus, I love you."

World in Sorrow

As word of her death spread, thousands of weeping people gathered in the rain outside her convent to pay homage to the humble, dedicated nun who had spent 68 years in India.

At his summer residence in Castel Gandolfo, Pope John Paul II spoke with a trembling voice as he expressed his grief. Rising early on Saturday morning, the pope celebrated a private Mass for the repose of the soul of his dear friend. A few hours later, in a public appearance, the pontiff told several thousand people how deeply he felt her death. "This morning I celebrated Mass with intimate emotion for her. She is an unforgettable witness to a love made up of concrete and ceaseless service to the poorest and most down-and-out people. Traveling ceaselessly the streets of the world, Mother Teresa marked the history of this century. With courage she defended life. She served every human being by always promoting dignity and respect."

From London, Queen Elizabeth voiced her "deep sadness" over the death of Mother Teresa. President William Clinton described her as an "incredible person." He recalled that just months earlier she had received the highest civilian honor bestowed by Congress. In the House of Representatives a moment of silence was observed in her memory.

In New Delhi, on Saturday, September 6, Prime Minister Inder Kumar Gujral ordered a state funeral for Mother Teresa, an honor normally conferred only on presidents and prime ministers. Flags flew at half-staff across India.

Funeral Services

The Mass of Christian Burial was celebrated on September 13, 1997 at Netaji Stadium, with the Vatican Secretary of State, Angelo Cardinal Sodano, as the main celebrant. The funeral procession began with six high-ranking Indian Army officers carrying Mother Teresa's coffin about one hundred yards to the waiting carriage from St. Thomas Church, where her body had been brought for public viewing on September 7. The procession then moved down Calcutta's main streets.

Concelebrating with Cardinal Sodano were four cardinals, about thirty bishops, and 170 priests from many countries.

Those to whom Mother Teresa had dedicated her life were represented in the offertory procession. An orphaned girl carried flowers, a woman released from prison carried the water, a leper carried the wine, and a handicapped person carried the bread for the Mass.

After the Mass, several celebrants sprinkled holy water on her casket. Following the blessing, a delegate of the Anglican Communion and representatives of Hindu, Islamic, Sikh, Buddhist and Parsi religions gave tribute to the Catholic nun whose understanding of love went far beyond religious distinctions.

Mother Teresa's Secret

One day Mother Teresa was asked to give a definition of herself. What kind of a person was she? What was her motivating power? How did she see herself as a follower of Christ? Her response: "By blood, I am an Albanian. I am a citizen of India. I am a Catholic and a religious. By vocation I belong to the whole world. But my heart belongs entirely to Jesus."

What was the secret of Mother Teresa's life? She may have revealed it herself when answering that question asked by a journalist.

"My secret is Jesus. His great love for us, prayer, daily meditation and adoration of the Blessed Sacrament, my religious vows. My motto is 'Everything for Jesus through Mary.' "

Commenting on the work of Mother Teresa, Pope John Paul II once paid a wonderful tribute to her. "Mother Teresa is today the most beautiful expression of Christian love at the service of life and of suffering humanity. We are called to such holiness. She has already fulfilled that call."

And when Mother Teresa said that her motto was "Everything for Jesus through Mary," she was reflecting her deep-seated love for the Blessed Mother. The rosary was always clasped in her hands, no matter where she was. Even in the presence of powerful world leaders, her rosary was her "security blanket." She used to tell her Sisters: "We can become saints with the help of Mary. Like her, let us be zealous in bringing Jesus to others. Like her, we can become 'full of grace' by receiving Holy Communion. Mary is the Queen of heaven and earth, the mediatrix of all the graces we receive. Pray to Mary and you will be sure to experience her love and help."

Joy in God's Work

The Biblical exhortation to "serve the Lord with joy," was certainly demonstrated in the life of Mother Teresa and her followers. She often told her Sisters that the "best way to show our gratitude to God and to others is to do everything with joy." Speaking of her religious congregation, she stated that: "Joy is an essential element of our religious society. A Missionary of Charity has to be a missionary of joy. By this spirit of joy will everyone recognize you as members of this Society. When people of the world see you at work, they admire not only the work you are doing, but even more your joyfulness in doing the work. By joy I mean that interior and profound serenity of the spirit which is in you, in your eyes, in your looks, in the attitude you show others in your work."

"God is joy. Jesus became man to bring us joy, the good news of redemption. Mary said, 'My spirit rejoices in God my Savior.' And the baby that Elizabeth was carrying leapt with joy because Mary brought him Christ. We receive the same Jesus in Holy Communion. Are the poor happy when they see us? Let us give them the living God, the God of joy."

"At Bethlehem everyone shared joy: the shepherds, the angels, the Magi, Joseph and Mary. And joy was the hallmark of the early Christians. Saint Paul exhorted the early Christians to 'be joyful in the Lord.' "

Teresa and Diana

When Princess Diana went to visit Mother Teresa in New York on June 18, 1997, the mass media had a field day covering the event. Here was a very popular and extremely beautiful princess. Next to her was a frail, diminutive nun, known and respected the world over for her work for the poorest of the poor. Both had endeared themselves to the world. Mother Teresa had gathered to her bosom the lepers and the dying from the slums of Calcutta. Diana had demonstrated great love for her two sons, embraced babies with AIDS, campaigned to abolish land mines, and to help people caught in the deadly grip of drug addiction. Exposure to a watching, wondering, and worshiping world was inevitable for Princess Diana and Mother Teresa.

When Malcolm Muggeridge, a distinguished British personality and writer, invited Mother Teresa to his studio for a TV interview for BBC, little did Mother Teresa know that her image would be telecast to half the British population. She was an ideal person to be interviewed: a Catholic nun from India, crowned with honors and awards for her life in Calcutta's slums, and loving care for those whom no one cared for throughout the world. The stage was set for a sensational interview. It was then that Mother Teresa exclaimed in all simplicity, "Let's do something beautiful for God."

It may never have dawned on this charismatic nun that "doing something beautiful for God" summed up her entire life. Her years as a Sister of Loreto, her departure from these Sisters and the founding of a new congregation, The Missionaries of Charity, her generous response to calls from bishops in many countries, the almost miraculous multiplication of her hospitals, clinics, leprosaria, and refuges for the poorest of the poor—all of these things were doing "something beautiful for God" for so many years.

She was not only the "Woman of the Year," but the "Woman of the Century."

Additional Titles Published by Resurrection Press, a Catholic Book Publishing Imprint

A Rachel Rosary Larry Kupferman	$4.50
Blessings All Around Dolores Leckey	$8.95
Catholic Is Wonderful Mitch Finley	$4.95
Come, Celebrate Jesus! Francis X. Gaeta	$4.95
From Holy Hour to Happy Hour Francis X. Gaeta	$7.95
Healing through the Mass Robert DeGrandis, SSJ	$9.95
Our Grounds for Hope Fulton J. Sheen	$7.95
The Healing Rosary Mike D.	$5.95
Healing Your Grief Ruthann Williams, OP	$7.95
Heart Peace Adolfo Quezada	$9.95
Life, Love and Laughter Jim Vlaun	$7.95
Living Each Day by the Power of Faith Barbara Ryan	$8.95
The Joy of Being a Catechist Gloria Durka	$4.95
The Joy of Being a Eucharistic Minister Mitch Finley	$5.95
The Joy of Being a Lector Mitch Finley	$5.95
The Joy of Being an Usher Gretchen Hailer, RSHM	$5.95
Lights in the Darkness Ave Clark, O.P.	$8.95
Loving Yourself for God's Sake Adolfo Quezada	$5.95
Personally Speaking Jim Lisante	$8.95
Practicing the Prayer of Presence van Kaam/Muto	$8.95
5-Minute Miracles Linda Schubert	$4.95
Season of New Beginnings Mitch Finley	$4.95
Season of Promises Mitch Finley	$4.95
Soup Pot Ethel Pochocki	$8.95
Stay with Us John Mullin, SJ	$3.95
Surprising Mary Mitch Finley	$7.95
Teaching as Eucharist Joanmarie Smith	$5.95
What He Did for Love Francis X. Gaeta	$5.95
You Are My Beloved Mitch Finley	$10.95
Your Sacred Story Robert Lauder	$6.95

For a free catalog call 1-800-892-6657